The Woman with Sandpaper Skin

And Other Poems

by Charday Ife

FOREIGN
· · · · · · · · · ·
NATIVE

FIRST EDITION

Published by Foreign Native

ISBN: 978-0-9986659-0-0

To the militant lovers,
All of the kings and queens
with their crowns in their closets,
All of the superheroes
with capes in their back pockets.

FORWARD

The Woman with Sandpaper Skin is a collection of poetry and prose from the coming of age of a brown girl, a little rough around the edges. This collection represents the cultivation of my bold inner voice; it serves to lift up the light present in the darkest of situations. The poetry included travels from my adolescent discovery of femininity, and grapples with my lessons in patience, freedom, and definitions of the divine. It represents my self-pep talks, affirmations and lived experiences. It is Black Girl Magic. As you read *The Woman with Sandpaper Skin*, I encourage you to take notes in the margins and the journal pages included, internalize affirmations, and highlight ways to invest in your continued luminosity.

her glow
is not to be seen with two eyes
her glory
deep-rooted in a past
not fond of the outcast

on midnight strolls,
she practices self-control
puts the "pro" in prodigy
the "disciple" in discipline
glides gracefully
hiding feet cut and bloodied

others brush up against her
and are softened by her touch
yet still view her as rough

gallant girl
turns
willful woman
unabashedly peaceful and positive
goes to and go gets it
the brown-skinned
coarse song in gentle wind

here's to youth
to whiskey in wine glasses
pigeons and doves
Snapchat documentaries
tattooed histories
and bottled grief

to the grown-up lines
etched into the
young girl's face

to maturity
nearly ten years into puberty
unmasking of virginity

coronations after king's cup playing
bones in ivory towers

to shot glasses turned ash trays skies
with stars we cannot see
city streets turned catwalks

to intoxicated confessions
and makeup covers

and wish books bursting with dreams

my father
gave me my eye
for the rebel type
    the men with voices
        like military salutes
        how chillingly commanding they are
            bootstraps tied
            luggage by the screen door
                how reflexive
                how ready they are
                men too cautious
                for institutions

urban seafarers with eyes like departing ships
they blink and are off again
men with voices like muffled thunder
                  I always prayed
                  to be your **anchor**
              come judgement day
              to be present
          when those sailors
          remove their boots
        rest their souls
        and find themselves
      satisfied
    after searching
    for home
    for so long

Letter to my 18-year-old self:

"Because it did (or didn't) feel right" is as valid a motivator as any.

You are equipped with a moral compass. Some things you feel powerfully, beyond a shadow of a doubt. This belief transcends the mental realm—it is the very particles you are composed of. Just as you cannot help but lose oxygen when thrown underwater, you cannot control the quickening of your heart or the calming of your muscles when certain people are in your presence.

Do not be afraid to embrace the unseen forces that move you. They are the reason your glands are healthily secreting, your knees are bending, and your nerve impulses activate. It is no wonder (and no problem) that love—one of the most powerful capacities humanity possesses—falls into that same category of visceral sensations.

Listen to the body you were created in. Revel in the delight that is being human. Rejoice at how lotion after water softens skin. Entertain only those who welcome your brilliance.

Start with the big tasks first. Teach yourself how to love. Then, teach the world, too.

dear God,
please excuse my hands for shaking
like the Earth is quaking at
my palm's fault lines

don't mind the sweat
rushing across the ridges in my fingers
like Gulf waters pouring over levees
I just want to get this right.

all my life,
I have felt Your presence in
the shiver of my spine

in the sense of security
You provide in adversity
in the
coincidences
subtle reminders of the
biggest blessings
that have ever come my way

I've seen You in the sway
of my grandmother's hips
as she fries fish
on Friday nights
saw you gazing at me
through my mother's eyes
I hear You
in my father's voice
I taste your mercy
in the salt of my tears
smell Your glory
when rain water hits dry
dirt

dear Lord,
I can feel your energy
vibrating in the core of me
like a stellar supernova nearing explosion
when I feel this
I'm convinced that Your Spirit envelops this earth
if ever I begin to question,
you hit me with a challenge
disguised as a blessing,
so I pray

I pray that You give me
hands to clasp,
and an ocean to watch
trails to blaze,
and problems to solve
feelings to sift,
and words for my thoughts
strong legs,
and moist Earth to run
across,
and a revolution for today
with no blood as the cost

for long
fear was my anthem

I slipped,
fell, c r a c k e d
my head open

the song stuck therein finally

came
        pouring
                out

Play musical chairs with your most cherished beliefs and completely rearrange all that you once thought to be fundamental. Redefine familiar. Call it something you never want to feel again. Do not fear yourself, nor that which you may morph into.

Re-conceptualize everything we can conceive of: friendships, upbringing, dreams, religion, sexuality, tastes, looks, voice, writing, accents, love, etc. Remain relevant and excited. Re-imagine yourself in a multitude of lights. Innovation is the key to longevity.

Learn the difference between distance and space.

Time will become irrelevant.

Life unfolds without notice of the number of times the sun rises and sets. Continue to dream, however long you are here. We are kept alive by weaving ever-more elaborate conceptions of ourselves.

I remember getting so mad at him that I would be able to taste it. Still, I wanted to present him with more of my insides—to vomit and spit my anger into his face. I wanted to use all of my strength and just crush his ribs—to show him that women are strong enough to, that I wasn't his slave, that nature didn't make me weak and subordinate, that me being a woman and he being a man didn't entitle him to anything.

At the same time, I believed that if I was affectionate enough, he would return the love. What I received in no way reflected what I had contributed. Instead, the man simply began to expect my unquestioning generosity.

I knew it was time to move on when I looked in the mirror and recognized how beautiful, bold, and self-aware I had become. I realized that although his obsession with me was justified, his mistreatment was not. It was not an easy process, for I was so conceited that I had no wish of denying any man my company.

sing
as if earth's gravity would wither
            without your melody

dream
as if God herself
            were your imagination

love
like snowflakes
            kissing the eyelashes of giants
 like gravel and nails
ground up
            sprinkled over bowls of rocky roads

rise
like ten thousand suns
            over the Alaskan tundra

shine
like the galactic confetti from the creation
            of the next universe's sun.

it was shoulder shrugs and light footsteps
averted gazes and
o n e
trying to feel like a pair

arabic
curved like the baker's smile
guidance toward the women's section
hijabs
blue as the Bosphorous
palaces
with wudu stations of glory
stone inscriptions and a warm place
sesame seed pretzels juxtaposed against
gutras
checkered red and white
finish lines
calligraphy
the desert-wanderers' path winding to
Cordoba
our history books forgot about ceilings
so dazzling that they dizzy
bazaars
merchant men's rainbows
embroidered boots
jeweled lamps
there is nothing shameful about extravagance
pistachios, pomegranates
apple tea,
spice shops, dervish figurines
in the land with fruit sweet enough to be dessert
the old wall crumbling
a message for the times:
Constantine rules here no more

cafeteria identity crises:
why do you wear that rag on your head?
what does your hair look like?
why don't you make your own triangle-shaped,
diagonal-cut lunches?
why do your sandwich bags fold over?
who are you?

to every religious rebel
who dares to call herself both
American and Muslim

who is brown-skinned, big-brained,
bigger bosomed, and beautiful:

show the world Allah's light
how when you smile
it glows
whether your hair is wrapped
or it shows

know that love is Love
and right is Right
regardless of whether your
father
brother
husband
uncle
tells you so

sometimes jealousy wears a cloak
dyed in power
to mask its shame

I am regal. I am the master of my temple.

I accept my God-given gifts.

I hereby declare acceptance of my weight, my hair, my eyes, and everything about my physical and emotional being.

I commit to always affirm my beautiful.

blasphemy

when you text me
"Good morning, beautiful"
I know you're really apologizing
for not being able to kiss my eyelids with the rising sun

when I respond "How are you?"
what I really want to know is whether that gargantuan
heart of yours still beats like 10,000 children's fists in
unison
banging at God's door

how could I ever ignore a touch that praised me?
or the Holy Ghost that possessed me
in between each of your
exhales?

you speak
and it's as if my blood carries
millions of microscopic
renditions of Moses's staff
that plunge themselves at my pores
goosebumps rising like it's Resurrection Day

we never sleep when we're together
but we sure as hell dream
conjurings vibrant as Joseph's robes
and I know you weren't foolish enough to think
that I would write a
mediocre love poem
for the man who led me to believe that
maybe Mary
had more to offer
than her virginity

there is Zion in your smile
the plumpness of your bottom lip
is reminiscent of fruits in the Garden of Eden
the gravel in your voice
sends rock slides to bury disbelievers
your displeasure is like brimstone showers

if ever you were to fall ill,
I'm certain you would cough up
plumes of volcanic ash
your sickness:
a divinely delivered natural disaster

your stories
are trumpets blaring at St. Peter's gate
our conversations
judgment day
minus the judgment
the span of the wings at your spine
makes the angels want to clip theirs
your smile
makes me want to write our story into the Bible
to prove to you that
as unorthodox as our love is
I still find
God
in it

noble as the Messenger
you refused to allow me to reveal to you my ticklish spots
explaining that you'd take your time to find them
like prophets
trekking desert sands in pursuit of peace
and the only thing you've professed
that I refuse to believe
is that you aren't a poet
for you scribble scripture into my skin
with hands heavy as thunder,
yet gentle as rain

the sound of your morning bones cracking
is like the Children of Israel
slow clapping
to the rhythm of your snores
the genesis
not even a goddess could ask for more

more gentle, more graceful
more patient, more able
more forehead kisses and midnight pecks
more smile-ridden arguments
more moonlight, more hands
more wrinkles, less plans
more sunshine, less fog
more godly, less God

who is there to uplift the downtrodden than
we who have seen
those allegorical bootstraps
strangle then snap necks?

apologies

I've got tears in my eyes
and a rainbow at my cheeks
there's gold in my smile
"I'm sorry"
was but a flake--
an unconcerned shrug
a meaningless sideways glance
an insincere apology
the sound of his heart breaking
like he choked on his dreams shattering
the echo of forever
pouring over a phone line
I just knew it
didn't feel right

nothing tasted sweeter than Goodbye
it was the sound of a cigarette carton
kissing the wastebasket
a milestone
a gold medal that only I could see
a symbol of how I learned to unapologetically be me
a deviation from conformity
a declaration of femininity
"Goodbye"
the beginning of
"I'm free"

There comes a time when things stand still. The change tumbling in beggars' cups ceases to echo, cars slow, my heartbeat drops to a soft thump, my lips remain pressed, and my list of desires is nonexistent.

I am where I would like to be. I want for near nothing and am emotionally stable. I have been working on self-improvement for one year and six months.

My "new year" always happens when the summer temperatures reach their zenith. Everything speeds by. Skateboarders takeover beach fronts, children race barefoot in streets releasing energy collected since winter, breaths quicken upon the realization that another milestone has been met. It is difficult to find something I would like to do differently today, January 1st. There is not anything happening. Not really. I am here listening to coins silently throw themselves against cups, hypnotized by the cars frozen on Flower Street.

I am by myself
in solitude and single
the only human in this whole house but I feel warmth
that rivals the inside of stomachs
on the last Thursday of November
 I hear silence
smooth as the summer ocean's surface I am inhaling air
thick
like the last breaths of my ancestors
today,
I am anything but alone

how could he set the scales straight if he never held weight?
he's got hormones disguised as lava boiling rage
deceptive
the system fed it to him that way

his heartbeat sounds like helicopter blades

cut the grass or leave it tall,
it's gon always be snakes

if the sun shine or rain pours,
it's gon always be shade

light is birthed in darkness

I am selfish for self-preservation, self-centered on greatness, and self-absorbed for the sake of my path.

red things bloom while the world is hot
loud tomato warnings
strawberry sirens
young blood's insides by the curbside like pie fillins
22-year-old father shot
created orphans out of three children
another of the sacrament's sacrificial killins
got me wonderin when
have conviction, not be convicted
we'll hail heroes and not victims
be vindicated and not vindictive
we'll erect a kingdom in this system

here in Sacramento
we've been cop watching
since hopscotching
we're used to dreadlocks
and mango Arizonas
we're used to pop-locking
and glocks stopping
the teen clubs
gangsta rap
and the occasional mean mug
basketball shorts
and that Omar Epps love

we've got talent
we've got hope
the generation just past dope
got it hard, but we gon cope
release that gospel from our souls
heal our people, let them know
that we put on for Sacramento

Life is about approaching daunting tasks with hope and good intentions. As much as we'd like to believe that right and wrong are cut and dry, the truth is, there's a bit of yin in every yang. There's gray area.

No matter how ardently I anticipate and recognize forthcoming trials, they will surprise me and bring me to my knees. It is not a symbol of weakness; it is a sign of the consistency in the cycle. Accept it. Get stronger. Believe always in the future. Look ahead with that same ambition. Be sure to pair it with action. Do not be discouraged. Meditate on the end goal and run after it. Sulking will only bring you more sorrows.

Patience requires an abundance of some element we have somewhere in our minds convinced ourselves is negative. Time. Distance. Characteristics. It calls for a re-imagining of them in order to flourish. Patience forces us to add our own push to karma, to fill our glasses with homemade lemonade, dip a hand into the cosmic pond and marble yin and yang. Finger paint destiny's door. Patience doesn't require passivity or lack of action. Conversely, it urges innovation.

I trust what comes to me.
I am exactly where I am supposed to be.

she
was moved by

a **flame** the size of a

tea light when it breathed

it burned like growing pains

like innocence peeking through

behind muddy clothes

after a long day

of play

friends are like planets
every one with her own orbit
bringing
signs
and seasons
my way

sometimes spirits
touch me deeper than prophets
but who is to say
they are not one and the same

remember:
there is value in mutation
in the flaws in man's equation
products of an amalgamated nation
love tough
do not be forsaken
of course there are cr ack s upon the pavement
of the path divinely sanctioned

sometimes life don't need a poem
it needs action
fists smacking
into the belly of the beast
bows drawn
in the valley of deceit

sometimes poems don't need the past
they need the present
without the gift wrapping
sitting in a corner, abandoned
for us to remember

it's okay to feel darkness from time to time
it was blackness
that we were born in
darkness
is the beginning of dreams

I caught my eye
        flirting with the curls
in the mirror
        reflecting on how
I came to love my **reflection**
        dancing without rhythm
in a dingy blue dress
        flaunting five feet of legs
legs that feared sunlight
        because a false god
told her it was sin
        the heat in my face
gospel
        that scripture could never teach

f r e e

        is a verb
it is standing in solitude
        side-stepping satan with certainty
baring teeth
        both as a welcome
        and a warning

                                        you look lost
          your dreadlocks
                          like the scarecrow's arms
your mind
is exactly
                    where it is supposed
to be

red brick
no one knows the roads I've travelled
in class
I carve new identities for myself
but I will always be
   black
to some

rid the tyrant from your mind
admission to disbelief
in a deadly regime
is as revolutionary
as overthrowing it
let no one
tell
you
otherwise

be brave step proudly
own every shudder
follow every wince with a smile
you are complete the inverse of
s o m e
men

let no one tell you that is absolute
do not swallow anyone else's truth

your husband may make you
feel whole
do not expect him to understand
what filling
c h a s m s feels like

sometimes womanhood burns
like wildfires and global warming
like the palms of mercenaries
like lamps of the wealthy

your fluid is the salve scorched men are praying for
the example set for eras, infinite scores

NOTES / JOURNAL

NOTES / JOURNAL

NOTES / JOURNAL

NOTES / JOURNAL

NOTES / JOURNAL

NOTES / JOURNAL

NOTES / JOURNAL

NOTES / JOURNAL

NOTES / JOURNAL

NOTES / JOURNAL

NOTES / JOURNAL

NOTES / JOURNAL

NOTES / JOURNAL

NOTES / JOURNAL

NOTES / JOURNAL

NOTES / JOURNAL

NOTES / JOURNAL

www.ingramcontent.com/pod-product-compliance
Lightning Source LLC
Chambersburg PA
CBHW060144050426
42448CB00010B/2290